Fuji

Empire

Cox

Jonagold

Cortland

Jazz

Idared

Golden Delicious

Red Delicious

McIntosh

Honeycrisp

Crispin

Royal Gala

Ginger Gold

Rome

Granny Smith

Macoun

Eating | Baking
Best for
Cooking | Juicing

Gala

Paula Red

Cameo

Braeburn

Jonathan

Apple Varieties*

Cripps Pink

Printed in the United States of America
ISBN: (p) 978-1-64250-744-7
(e) 978-1-64250-745-4
www.mangopublishinggroup.com
www.flavcity.com

The Tasty Adventures
of Rose Honey
CINNAMON APPLE CAKE

by Bobby & Dessi Parrish
Cowritten and Illustrated
by Kaloyan Nachev & Boril Nachev

Rose Honey was snuggled in bed on a crisp fall morning. She dreamed of a magical orchard in a faraway land. The trees were heavy with sweet, juicy apples and Rose picked the ripest ones to fill her basket.

When she awoke, she knew just what she wanted to do.
She jumped out of bed and ran into the kitchen.
"Mommy, let's make apple cake!"
"How about cinnamon apple cake with caramel sauce?"
asked Mommy. "Full of yummy spices and nuts!"

Daddy cut the apples into perfect thin slices. To Rose they looked like teeny-tiny boats that could sail across an ocean of apple juice.

Rose looked down and saw a little bottle floating on the surface. She opened it, and the sweet warming scent of cinnamon carried her to a distant and magical place. It was the land of spices and aromas.

Rose found herself at the spice market. It was filled with swirls of colors and scents, and the aromas tickled her nose. Rose jumped inside a colorful plate and it took her on a magical ride above the bazaar.

Cumin Seeds

Sesame Seeds

Nutmeg

Fennel

Apple Tea

Black Cardamom

Cloves

Juniper

Cardamom

Walnuts

"Mommy, what other spices do we need for the apple cake?"
"Cloves and nutmeg," said Mommy. Rose grabbed some
sweet and spicy cloves and some earthy nutmeg.

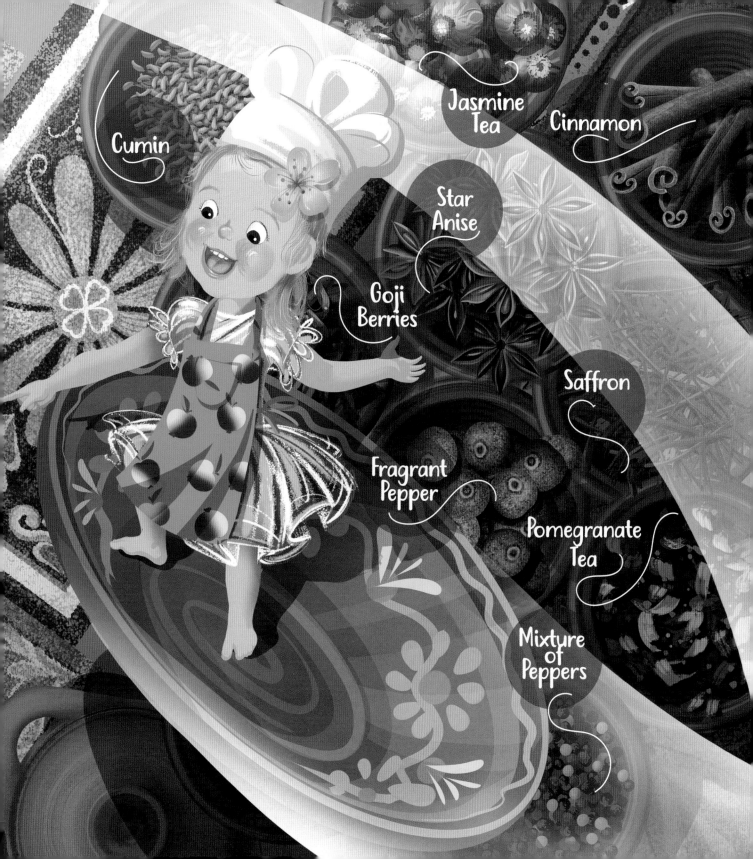

"Mommy, I got all the spices we need for the cake!" Rose Honey declared. "Perfect," said Mommy. "Let's add them to the almond flour mix." Stir, stir, stir! Mmmmm, the warming smell of spices filled the air.

ALMOND FLOUR

Rose couldn't help but sneak a taste of the coconut sugar. She found the nutty caramel flavor irresistible. Together, they combined the eggs with the coconut sugar and vanilla then beat them into a fluffy mixture.

"Let's add coconut oil," said Mommy.
"It will make the cake moist and luscious."

Next, Rose helped Daddy grate the apples. They squeezed the juice and she drank it all! It was sweet and yummy.

Mommy mixed in the apples and poured the batter into a baking pan. Rose sprinkled some toasted walnuts on top.

Mommy put the cake in the roaring hot oven and Rose set the hourglass. Soon, the scent of toasty nuts, vanilla, and spices was everywhere.

While the cake was baking, there was still work to be done.
"We have just enough time to make the caramel sauce!" Daddy said.
Coconut milk, coconut sugar, and a few pinches of salt simmered
in a pan, until it turned into a delicious, silky sauce.

The last grain of sand fell down and the cake was done.
Daddy said, "Ready or not, here we come!" and pulled
the scrumptious treasure out of the oven.
Rose poured the velvety caramel sauce all over it.

Rose was in the kitchen once again. The wind carried the smell
of the cinnamon apple cake to the faraway land.
This cake granted wishes.

And when Rose Honey tasted it, she found herself right back in the land of spices and aromas, flying on her magic plate.

Apple Crumble

Baked Apple

Baked Charlotte

Baked Flapjack

Apple Juice

Apple Pie

As Rose went to bed that night, she wished that her tasty adventures would never end.

And she dreamed of all the yummy apple desserts she wanted to make next.

Toffee Apple Pudding

Tarte Tatin

Apple Compote

Apple Strudel

Apple Pie Ice Cream

Stuffed Apple

Cinnamon Apple Cake

INGREDIENTS:

For the Cake:

2 cups (190g) blanched almond flour
½ cup (64g) arrowroot starch or tapioca starch
2 teaspoons (10g) ground cinnamon
½ teaspoon (2.5g) ground cloves
½ teaspoon (2.5g) grated nutmeg
2 teaspoons (10g) baking powder
1 pinch salt
3 eggs
2 egg whites
1 cup (140g) coconut sugar
1 teaspoon (5ml) vanilla paste or extract
¾ cup (178ml) virgin coconut oil, melted
1 cup (120g) peeled and grated apples
     (about 2 medium sized apples
     (Honey Crisp, Gala or Fuji))
¾ cup (100g) toasted and chopped walnuts

For the Caramel Sauce:

1 can (13.5 oz/400ml) full fat coconut milk
½ cup (70g) coconut sugar
2 pinches salt
1 teaspoon (5ml) vanilla extract

PREP TIME: 20 MINUTES
COOKING TIME: 40 MINUTES
MAKES: 8 SERVINGS

Watch Rose Honey make this delicious apple cake!

DIRECTIONS:

Preheat oven to 375°F (190°C).

In a large bowl, add the almond flour and arrowroot starch along with the ground cinnamon, ground cloves, grated nutmeg, baking powder and a pinch of salt. Mix well.

In a separate bowl, use a hand mixer to beat the eggs and egg whites on high along with the coconut sugar and vanilla until fluffy and the sugar is completely dissolved, about 3 minutes. Add the melted coconut oil and mix to combine.

Pour the egg mixture on top of the flour mixture and beat on medium until well combined.

Peel and grate the apples and squeeze out all of the excess juice. Measure one cup of the grated and squeezed apples and add it to the batter.
Mix well and pour into a 9-inch (23cm) round springform baking pan lined on the bottom with parchment paper.

Top the batter with the toasted and chopped walnuts.

Bake in a 375°F (190°C) oven for 38 to 40 minutes or until inserted toothpick comes out clean. The edges of the cake should be deep brown in color.

For the caramel sauce, place the coconut milk, coconut sugar and a couple of pinches of salt in a small pot and bring to a boil.

Turn the heat down to low and simmer on low for about 40 to 50 minutes while stirring occasionally with a wooden spoon. The sauce will reduce and turn a deep caramel color. It's done when it coats the back of the spoon.

Keep in mind that it will thicken a little more once it cools down.
Remove from the heat, stir in the vanilla extract and set aside to cool.

This recipe makes about 8oz (235ml) of caramel sauce.
Once both cake and sauce have cooled down, drizzle the caramel sauce all over the cake and serve!

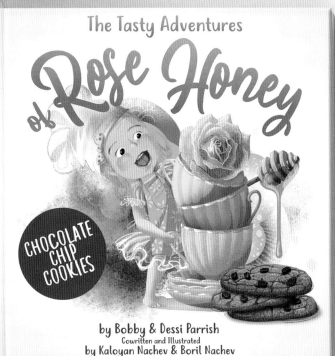

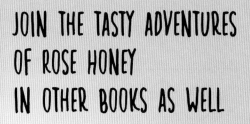

CHOCOLATE AVOCADO PUDDING

While making her special chocolate pudding, Rose finds out about the magic of growing up and how a little seed can turn into a big tree.

CHOCOLATE CHIP COOKIES

Rose Honey loves cooking and baking with Mommy and Daddy. Chocolate chip cookies are one of her favorite treats and making them is an adventure for little Rose. Join her on this magical culinary journey.

ABOUT THE AUTHORS

Bobby and Dessi are bestselling cookbook authors with millions of followers across the world. With his popular FlavCity videos, Bobby shares grocery shopping and healthy food tips. Bobby's favorite place is in the kitchen, making delicious meals for his family.

Dessi dedicates her time to raising their daughter, Rose Honey. She also enjoys paleo baking, doing food photography, and painting.

Rose loves being involved in everything Mom and Dad do, especially in the kitchen where she helps make all kinds of tasty dishes. You can find all of Rose Honey's cooking videos on the FlavCity Facebook page. www.facebook.com/flavcity

ABOUT THE ILLUSTRATORS

Kaloyan Nachev, the illustrator and cowriter of this book, is also Dessi's brother. He is an acclaimed artist, producer, director, and screenwriter. He lives in Bulgaria where Dessi is originally from. Kaloyan has four children and loves spending time with his family. His oldest son, Boril Nachev, helped cowrite and illustrate this book. Kaloyan adores his niece Rose Honey and has a special connection with her, as she was born just a few days after his youngest daughter Petra.

Fuji

Empire

Cox

Jonagold

Cortland

Jazz

Idared

Golden Delicious

Red Delicious

McIntosh

Honeycrisp

Crispin

Royal Gala

Ginger Gold

Rome

Granny Smith

Macoun

Eating | Baking
Best
for
Cooking | Juicing

Gala

Paula Red

Cameo

Braeburn

Jonathan

Apple
Varieties*

Cripps Pink